It's Just the Way I Talk

Facts About Stuttering
for Ages 5-8

Jennifer
Tillock
M.S. CCC-SLP

Mrs. Speech
BOOKS

For all the Kids who stutter, and those that love them.

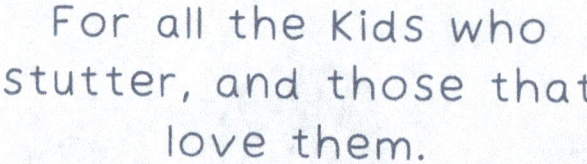

E-Book ISBN: 979-8-9906153-5-9
Print ISBN: 979-8-9906153-6-6

What is stuttering?

Stuttering is when you have a hard time getting words out.

Kinds of Stuttering

Stuttering might feel like bumpy speech, where you say the same sound again.

It may feel like your throat is locked, or the words are stuck.

Everyone stutters differently

Some kids stutter a lot, some only stutter a little.

Some only have bumpy speech. Some kids have lots of stuck words.

How Others Act

Other people who don't stutter may not Know what is happening.

They may want to help, but don't Know what to do.

What Others May Say

They may look nervous.

They may tell you to do things like "Slow down," or "Just relax".

They may try to finish your sentences.

Helping isn't always helpful

They are trying to help, but it may make it harder to talk.

You may get frustrated, or even mad or embarrassed.

You can tell them what helps you.

Your speech pathologist, sometimes called a speech teacher or speech therapist, can help you Know what to say.

Others can help by...

Giving you all of their attention when you speak.

Letting you Know before they ask you to talk.

Letting you talk without interrupting.

Not rushing you to talk.

Treating you like everyone else.

Sometimes you stutter, sometimes you don't.

You might stutter more some times than other times.

Some people may be easier to talk to than others.

Singing may be super easy.

Stuttering changes

You may stutter more at home or at school.

Sometimes kids stutter more when they are excited or upset.

Stuttering can be a surprise.

Some kids have a hard time with certain sounds or words.

Sometimes you may not know when you are going to stutter.

Stay calm

If you try too hard to keep talking, you can make it harder.

Your face may get tight. You may start to do unusual things with your mouth or your face, like blinking hard.

What to do when you stutter

It is best to just let the stutter happen.

Don't try to stop it or hide it. Stuttering is OK.

Your speech pathologist can help you learn tricks that might make things easier, like using smooth starts.

Stuttering is OK

It's not your fault that you stutter.

It just happens, like a hiccup. It is OK to stutter.

Why do I stutter?

People who stutter have
brains that work
differently.

It's not because you are
nervous or scared.

It's just how your brain
works!

How did it happen to me?

Some families have the same hair color or eye color. Sometimes the way kids talk can be similar in families too!

If you stutter, someone in your family might have stuttered as a kid, too.

7 out of 10

Around 70% of adults who stutter have a family member who stutters

Facts about stuttering

- Stuttering is not caused by something bad that happened to you.
- Stuttering does not mean that you are not smart.
- Stuttering may not go away completely, even with therapy.
- Stuttering does not mean you are nervous.
- Stuttering does not mean you aren't working hard to use your strategies.

You are not the only one!

You are not the only Kid who stutters. Lots of other Kids stutter.

Grown-ups stutter too!

3,000,000

Three million people stutter
in the United States.
That's a really big number!

Three million
house flies would
weigh about as
much as a large
jaguar.

5 to 10 out of 100

5 to 10 percent of all children stutter at some time.

2 or 3 to 1

Boys are two
to three times
as likely to
stutter as girls

1 out of 4

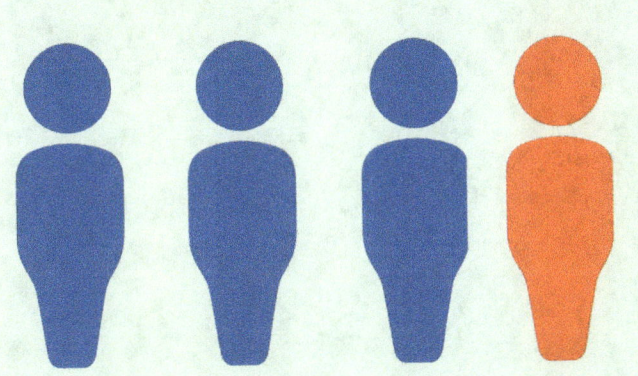

25% of kids who stutter will continue to stutter as adults.

You can do a lot of amazing things!

Maybe you are really good at a sport, or at making friends.

Maybe you are good at math, drawing, or telling stories.

No matter what, your friends and family love you because you are you!

What you can do about stuttering

Smooth Speech
Stretch out the bumps.

Take pauses.
Use periods and commas to take a breath and "reset."

Light contact.
Make your tongue and lips soft, instead of hard.

Therapy

A speech pathologist (SLP), also called a speech teacher or speech therapist, can help you come up with strategies that help you.

They can help you learn and practice those ideas, so they are easier to use.

What is therapy like?

- Fun Games: Your speech teacher will play fun games with you that help you practice talking smoothly. They may call it turtle talk or snail speech. They might ask you to stutter on purpose!

- Tricks: They can also teach you some 'tricks', or strategies, for talking that can help you stutter easier.

- Practice Makes Progress: Just like learning how to ride a bike, practicing these tricks will help you be able to use them easier.

Using strategies

It may make you tired to try to use strategies all the time.

It's okay to take a break, and just talk.

Remember, this is just how some kids talk.

Want to meet other kids who stutter?

Sometimes it feels good to talk to others who stutter. There are probably other kids in your school who stutter. You can ask your teacher or therapist to help you set up a group.

There are also stuttering groups in the community. Ask your parent if there is one near you.

Remember, it is ok to stutter.
It is just another way to talk.

Notes to teachers and parents

Tips for helping a child who stutters:

- Don't try to give advice unless it is a practice time.
- Show that you are listening actively, and give them time to talk.
- Keep natural eye contact.
- Be aware that some situations are harder than others.
- Speak in an unhurried, natural way.
- Be aware that stuttering can increase or decrease from day to day, even year by year.
- Help your child decide what works and what doesn't.
- Give advance notice of high stress speaking situations, like being asked to answer a question.
- Show that stuttering is OK. Avoid words like "bad," "worse" or "wrong" when you are talking about stuttering. Talk about it as normal and natural, like an accent or a hiccup.
- Focus on communication, not fluency. The goal is communicating easily, without fear of stuttering, not an absence of stuttering.

Online resources for teachers and parents

- The National Stuttering Association (NSA): https://westutter.org/
  - Offers a wealth of information on stuttering, including support groups, resources, and a "Back-to-School Survival Guide" for parents.
- The Stuttering Foundation: https://www.stutteringhelp.org/
  - Provides information on stuttering therapy, dealing with teasing, and building self-esteem in children who stutter. They also offer brochures and resources on fluency for parents and teachers.
- FRIENDS: The National Association of Young People Who Stutter: https://www.friendswhostutter.org/
  - A fantastic resource for young people who stutter, offering online support groups, conferences, and a sense of community.
- The American Speech-Language-Hearing Association (ASHA): https://www.asha.org/public/speech/disorders/stuttering/
  - Offers information on finding a qualified speech-language pathologist (SLP) who specializes in stuttering therapy.

About the Author

Jennifer Tillock is a speech-language pathologist with over 24 years of experience working with school-age children. She is currently a teletherapist who spends her spare time creating materials for other educators.

You can find her at MrsSpeechOnline.blogspot.com

Graphics by:
GraphicsRF on Canva

Talk It Out, Work It Out! A Safety & Self-Advocacy Workbook for Ages 8+

This book is designed to help kids 8+ to navigate challenges like stranger danger and social situations. It goes beyond scenarios by providing realistic tips, visual organizers, and a dedicated guide for parents and educators.

It's Just the Way I Talk: Facts About Stuttering for Ages 5-8
(Mrs. Speech Books)

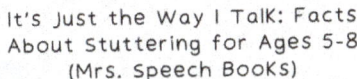

This book empowers children who stutter by explaining the condition in a positive way, offering strategies for managing it, and assuring them they're not alone. It also provides helpful tips for parents and teachers on how to best support children who stutter.

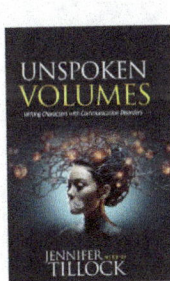

Unspoken Volumes: Writing Characters with Communication Challenges

This guide goes beyond stereotypes, offering insights from a therapist and empathy-building exercises. Practical tools like breakdowns and prompts help you write diverse characters and celebrate their stories.

Conversation Tennis Match: A Social Story
(Mrs. Speech Books)

Introducing a social story that uses the analogy of a tennis match to explain how conversations work, allowing children to grasp the concept of turn-taking and mutual exchange more easily. Includes ideas for additional activities in the classroom.

Why Do I Have To Work In A Group?
(Mrs. Speech Books)

This book addresses a common student complaint head-on. It not only outlines the benefits of group work but also offers practical tips for successful collaboration. From enhancing teamwork skills to fosterin creativity, this resource equips students with the tools they need to excel in group settings. Engage your students and transform their attitudes toward group projects with this invlauable resource.

Treasure Clues for Learning: Exploring Alternatives to "I Don't Know"
(Mrs. Speech Books)

This book offers kids 12 alternatives to "I don't know" to encourage student engagement and exploration. It provides the "why" behind these alternatives and how to use them effectively, turning classrooms into spaces where students feel empowered to learn.